COOL CARS

TESLA

BY DALTON RAINS

WWW.APEXEDITIONS.COM

Copyright © 2026 by Apex Editions, Mendota Heights, MN 55120. All rights reserved. No part of this book may be reproduced or utilized in any form or by any means without written permission from the publisher.

Apex is distributed by North Star Editions:
sales@northstareditions.com | 888-417-0195

Produced for Apex by Red Line Editorial.

Photographs ©: Pexels, cover; Shutterstock Images, 1, 4–5, 9, 10–11, 14, 16–17, 18, 19, 20–21, 26, 27, 29; Sergei Bulkin/TASS/ZUMA Press/Newscom, 6–7; SpaceX/Getty Images News/Getty Images, 12–13; Brandon Bell/Getty Images News/Getty Images, 15; Dylan Stewart/Image of Sport/Newscom, 22–23; Anne Chadwick Williams/PepsiCo Beverages North America/AP Images, 24–25

Library of Congress Control Number: 2025930933

ISBN
979-8-89250-527-7 (hardcover)
979-8-89250-563-5 (paperback)
979-8-89250-634-2 (ebook pdf)
979-8-89250-599-4 (hosted ebook)

Printed in the United States of America
Mankato, MN
082025

NOTE TO PARENTS AND EDUCATORS

Apex books are designed to build literacy skills in striving readers. Exciting, high-interest content attracts and holds readers' attention. The text is carefully leveled to allow students to achieve success quickly. Additional features, such as bolded glossary words for difficult terms, help build comprehension.

TABLE OF CONTENTS

CHAPTER 1
MODEL S PLAID 4

CHAPTER 2
HISTORY 10

CHAPTER 3
MAIN MODELS 16

CHAPTER 4
MANY MORE TESLAS 22

COMPREHENSION QUESTIONS • 28
GLOSSARY • 30
TO LEARN MORE • 31
ABOUT THE AUTHOR • 31
INDEX • 32

CHAPTER 1

MODEL S PLAID

Two cars line up for a **drag race**. One is a flashy Lamborghini. The other looks like a normal car. It's a Tesla Model S Plaid.

The Tesla Model S Plaid first hit the roads in 2021.

The Tesla shoots to a quick lead. It's a blur on the racetrack. The Lamborghini can't catch up.

The name "Plaid" comes from a superfast speed in the movie *Spaceballs*.

SUPERFAST

The Model S Plaid has three electric motors. They help the car accelerate. It can reach 60 miles per hour (97 km/h) in just under two seconds. That's faster than nearly any other **production car**.

The Model S Plaid crosses the finish line far ahead. The fully electric Tesla showed its speed. It's one of the fastest cars in the world.

FAST FACT

The Model S Plaid can go more than 200 miles per hour (322 km/h).

The Model S Plaid uses a yoke instead of a steering wheel. That's what aircraft use, too.

CHAPTER 2

History

Tesla was founded in 2003. The company's first project was the Roadster. The sports car came out in 2008.

In 2008, the Tesla Roadster could go 245 miles (394 km) on one charge.

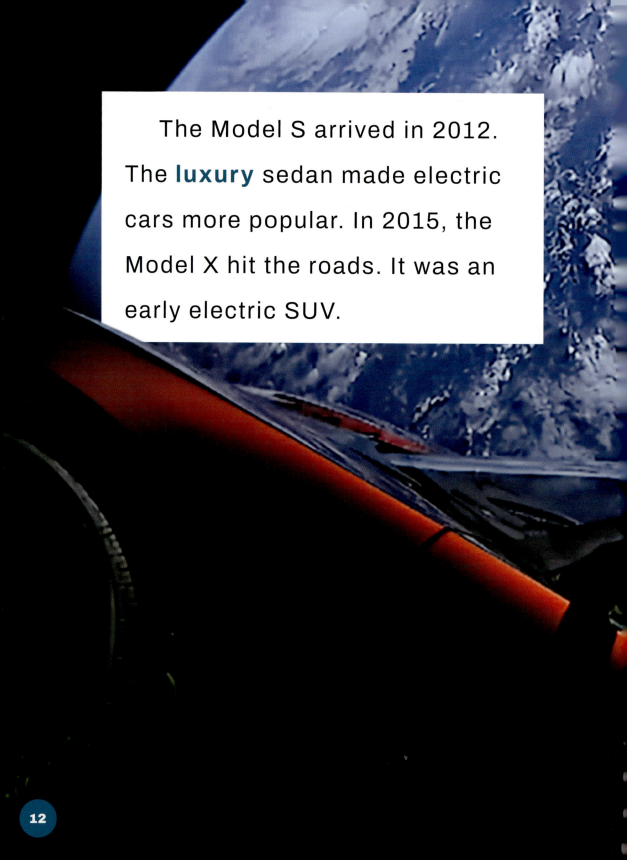

The Model S arrived in 2012. The **luxury** sedan made electric cars more popular. In 2015, the Model X hit the roads. It was an early electric SUV.

FAST FACT

Elon Musk helped fund Tesla in the early 2000s. Then he became its CEO in 2008.

In 2018, Elon Musk launched a rocket carrying his Tesla Roadster into space. A figure was put in the car to look like a driver.

Tesla began selling the Model 3 in 2017. It became the first electric car to reach one million sales.

The Model 3 came next. From 2018 to 2021, it was the world's best-selling electric car. Tesla had become an iconic car **brand**.

BATTERY POWER

Before Tesla, electric cars used expensive batteries. Tesla used batteries similar to what laptops and phones had. These batteries were cheaper. They were easier to charge, too.

Tesla has huge factories. Its headquarters in Texas covers 2,500 acres (1,000 ha).

CHAPTER 3

MAIN MODELS

Most early electric cars were small and slow. Tesla's Model S changed that. The car was quick and powerful. It had comfy seats and lots of room.

The Model S could go a similar distance on one charge as many gas-powered cars could on a full tank.

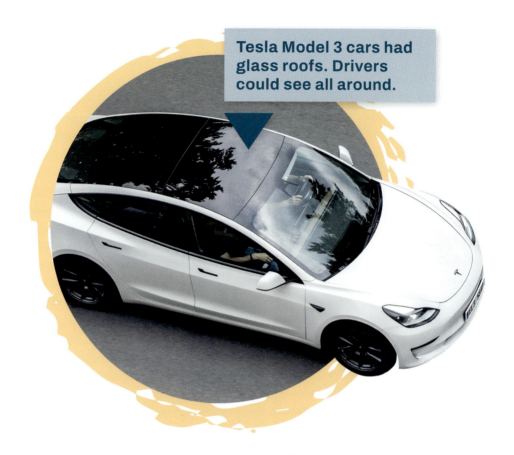

Tesla Model 3 cars had glass roofs. Drivers could see all around.

The Model 3 helped make electric cars more affordable. But it still had a sleek **design**. It had high-tech features, too. Some helped with safety. Others were for entertainment.

CHARGING UP

Tesla built charging stations across the world. They made long road trips easier. Stations also offered games and movies. Drivers could have fun while their cars charged.

Tesla's charging stations were called superchargers. By 2024, the company had 60,000 superchargers around the world.

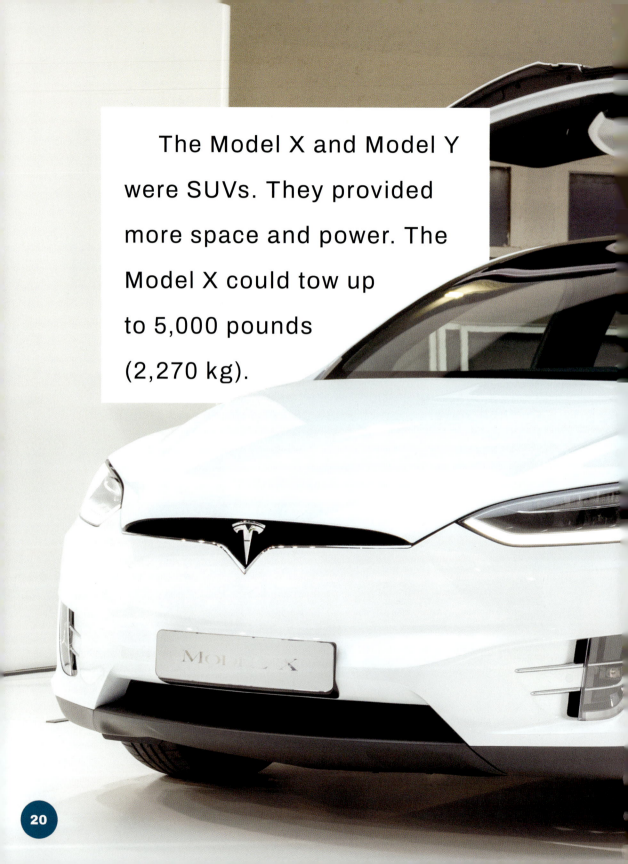

The Model X and Model Y were SUVs. They provided more space and power. The Model X could tow up to 5,000 pounds (2,270 kg).

A Model X's rear doors swung up to open.

FAST FACT

Many Teslas come in Plaid versions. These versions are extra fast and sporty.

21

CHAPTER 4

MANY MORE TESLAS

Tesla showed off a new Roadster in 2017. It was a **prototype**. The company spent years improving the sports car.

Tesla worked to make its new Roadster much faster than the original.

In 2022, Tesla delivered its first Semi. The **semitruck** could drive 500 miles (800 km) on one charge. It could pull 82,000 pounds (37,000 kg).

PepsiCo was one of the first companies to begin using Tesla Semis.

Autopilot

Autopilot came out in 2015. The **software** had self-driving features. But Autopilot wasn't perfect. It caused accidents. Tesla kept working on the technology.

The Cybertruck was strong. It could handle rough roads and extreme weather.

The Cybertruck came out in 2023. The truck's body was smooth steel. It had a bold, blocky shape. Fans looked forward to the next game-changing Tesla.

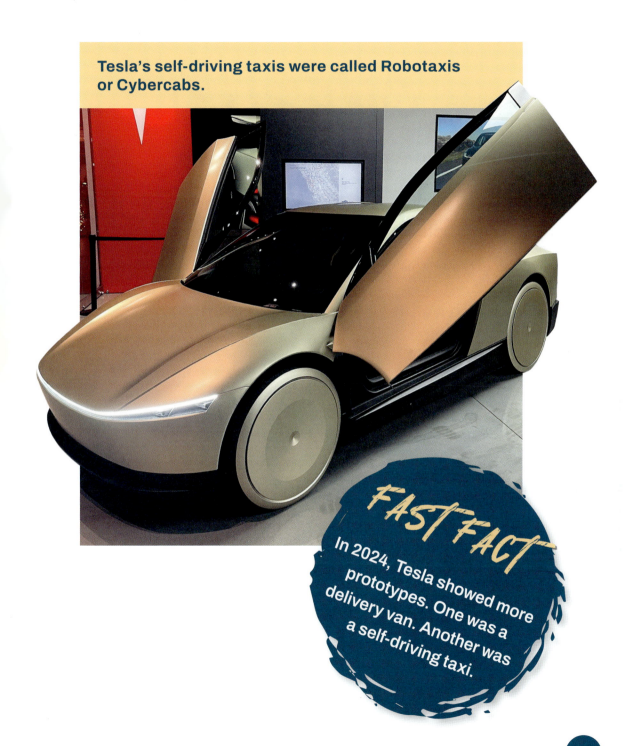

Tesla's self-driving taxis were called Robotaxis or Cybercabs.

FAST FACT

In 2024, Tesla showed more prototypes. One was a delivery van. Another was a self-driving taxi.

COMPREHENSION QUESTIONS

Write your answers on a separate piece of paper.

1. Write a few sentences explaining the main ideas of Chapter 2.

2. Which Tesla would you most like to have? Why?

3. When was Tesla founded?
    - A. 2003
    - B. 2008
    - C. 2012

4. Why might building many superchargers help make long road trips in Teslas easier?
    - A. Drivers could get new Teslas there if their cars broke.
    - B. Superchargers offered gas for Teslas when their batteries died.
    - C. Drivers had more places to stop and charge their Teslas' batteries.

5. What does **accelerate** mean in this book?

*They help the car **accelerate**. It can reach 60 miles per hour (97 km/h) in just under two seconds.*

- **A.** to stop moving
- **B.** to change direction
- **C.** to speed up

6. What does **iconic** mean in this book?

*From 2018 to 2021, it was the world's best-selling electric car. Tesla had become an **iconic** car brand.*

- **A.** only used long ago
- **B.** liked by many people
- **C.** unknown to most people

Answer key on page 32.

GLOSSARY

brand
The products and services connected with one company.

design
The way something looks or is made.

drag race
A race between two cars on a straight track.

luxury
Having to do with things that are high quality, comfortable, and often expensive.

production car
A car sold to the public and allowed to drive on public roads.

prototype
An early form of something, usually for testing.

semitruck
A truck that has a tractor part and a trailer part. The driver and engine are in the tractor. The trailer carries huge loads.

software
The programs that run on a computer and perform certain functions.

TO LEARN MORE

BOOKS

Colby, Jennifer. *Tesla*. Cherry Lake Publishing, 2023.
Respicio, Mae. *Sports Cars of Tomorrow*. Capstone Press, 2025.
Rusick, Jessica. *Electric Cars*. Abdo Publishing, 2024.

ONLINE RESOURCES

Visit **www.apexeditions.com** to find links and resources related to this title.

ABOUT THE AUTHOR

Dalton Rains is a writer and editor from St. Paul, Minnesota.

A
Autopilot, 25

B
batteries, 15

C
charging stations, 19
Cybertruck, 26

D
delivery van, 27
drag race, 4, 6–8

E
electric motors, 7

M
Model 3, 14, 18
Model S, 12, 16
Model X, 12, 20
Model Y, 20
Musk, Elon, 13

P
Plaid versions, 4, 6–8, 21
prototypes, 22, 27

R
Roadster, 10, 22

S
Semi, 24

ANSWER KEY:
1. Answers will vary; 2. Answers will vary; 3. A; 4. C; 5. C; 6. B